I0171760

Silent Throbs & Fractured Echoes

Maya Jaiswal

BookLeaf
Publishing

India | USA | UK

Copyright © Maya Jaiswal
All Rights Reserved.

This book has been self-published with all reasonable efforts taken to make the material error-free by the author. No part of this book shall be used, reproduced in any manner whatsoever without written permission from the author, except in the case of brief quotations embodied in critical articles and reviews.

The Author of this book is solely responsible and liable for its content including but not limited to the views, representations, descriptions, statements, information, opinions, and references ["Content"]. The Content of this book shall not constitute or be construed or deemed to reflect the opinion or expression of the Publisher or Editor. Neither the Publisher nor Editor endorse or approve the Content of this book or guarantee the reliability, accuracy, or completeness of the Content published herein and do not make any representations or warranties of any kind, express or implied, including but not limited to the implied warranties of merchantability, fitness for a particular purpose.

The Publisher and Editor shall not be liable whatsoever...

Made with ❤ on the BookLeaf Publishing Platform
www.bookleafpub.in
www.bookleafpub.com

Dedication

To my beloved parents, Smt. Sunita Devi and Shri Gopal Prasad Jaiswal. They made my journey worthwhile and helped me feel the vibrancy of poetry. My book, "*Silent Throbs & Fractured Echoes*", is born from their unsung tale of love and deep affection.

Preface

When I started gathering my poems in recent years, I was in a difficult place. I lived alone, in what felt like a cage, overwhelmed by constant pain. My half-breathing words were my only companions. I felt lost, not knowing where my path lay. I simply poured my heart onto the page. From *Your Footprints* to *My Inner Reeds* and *Ripples* to *My Fragile Bliss,* the poems held all the colors of life, love, sadness, joy and gratitude but I couldn't find a true release. My art was the one thing that kept me going.

I was fortunate to have great mentors who opened my eyes to richer possibilities. V Satheesan Sir (late) and Padma Shri Vijay Sharma Sir gave me the brush and the courage to paint my own canvas. Satheesan Sir's sudden death left a profound emptiness, and for many months, I struggled to recover. In that time, I wrote and read whenever the pain subsided. I was suffering, both spiritually and physically, from chronic cervical pain and emotional distress.

Joining the Directorate of Education as an arts teacher was a new beginning. I hoped to grow with my students, who came from various backgrounds. Working with differently-abled students, I tried to paint my own feelings. I found myself drawn to Kangra and Basohali art, and like O. Henry's masterpiece, *The Last Leaf*, I was waiting for my own artistic renaissance.

During this period, as I wrote about my *"Silent Throbs & Fractured Echoes"*, my mentor, Mr. Kamal Akhtar Sir, offered a new perspective. He saw something special in my work. He encouraged me to write about any expression that moved me, singling out lines like *"Flowers of my eyes not falling for fragrance"* and "*Certain peacocks drenching in sobbing rain*". He urged me to read widely, and I immersed myself in the wisdom of Keats, Donne, Marlowe, T.S. Eliot, W.H. Auden, Simon Armitage, Meena Kandasamy, and Anjum Hasan.

Empowered by this guidance, I shaped my poetry into its final form. Mr. Kamal Akhtar Sir graciously reviewed my poems and offered his invaluable suggestions. It is with his support that I now present this collection to you. Your reception of these poems will guide my future path. I have written them without adherence to any specific rhythm or meter, they are simply my silent throbs, echoing my fractured emotions for you to hear.

MAYA JAISWAL

Acknowledgements

This book of poetry owes its existence to many people. My Foremost, gratitude is to my parents, Smt. Sunita Devi and Shri Gopal Prasad Jaiswal, for their unending inspiration and blessings.
I would also like to express my profound thanks to V Satheesan Sir (late) and Padma Shri Vijay Sharma Sir for opening up a world of creativity to me. My siblings, Mrs. Kalyani, Ms. Bharti and Mr. Aditya have been the pillars of strength through all of life's ups and downs, and their influence is visible throughout my poetic development.

A special note of appreciation goes to Mr. Vishal Vishwakarma. His words of wisdom guided me through silent zones and helped overcome creative blocks. He also conceptualized the cover page.

Finally, I am deeply indebted to my Mentor, Mr. Kamal Akhtar Sir, whose guidance and inspired poetic deliberations helped me in shaping my original voice and crafting the book's title, "*Silent Throbs & Fractured Echoes*".

Your Grain

*Smoking ashes
passing through eyes,
My head
lying on floor
in the ice.*

*Crushed smiles
with red blood,
My nerves
flowing into flood.*

*The numbness of
nails,
Creating galaxy
in veils.*

*As in the stage of
paralyzed brain,
My soul
still recalls you*

and your magestic grain.

Rising Faith

An orb chosen for rebirth
emerged in the pond of
torn tears,
An ocean boat
descended to redeem it
upon the crooning pillars.

When the chrysalis faith
was decaying
inside the drop,
The sea speck
soothed it with love
and gifted a golden crop.

Gospium Tree

Pouring my entity into an empty vessel,
Putting my thoughts on a rough rigid castle.

Buds of sludge downside,
Worms of wood on high pride.

Both the banks undermined,
The Adam's Ale lost its holy wine.

Aquatics inhaling thirsty notes,
Optima leading to venomous throats.

Legend of anxoa climbing a top,
A cherub holding roots with a wishful hop.

Scarcity growing inch by inch,
Floras arising pinch by pinch.

A glaring shine upon the buds,
Turning it into diamond studs.

Grubs making the castle free,
Turning into a gospium tree.

A Kilmich' bursting out from a cotton plant,
With godly grain gifting a grant.

Vital Whirling

A creeper dug a hole
Allowing entry to a lonesome mole
While blood was soaked
And brain got stroked
Phalanges got numb
And ears went dumb
A wave of life quite curling
Taught me a vital whirling.

Where Faith Meets The Hidden

Secrecy of impassioned emotions
corrodes the heart of
forlorn penguins,
If faith exists nowhere
one would die for
cold-blooded mountains.

who would love with
sorrow deep inside
and handle the cracks of
leaves for no reason,
Degrees of falsehood
may change
yet falseness will remain.

One is made of
nerves in the brain
another born of
divine genes,

What kind of bond would that be
if it couldn't make
a white horse.

Porous Fingers

O' Melancholy!
Embrace me in your arm,
Let me settle down
Tracing the lines of your palm.

Tell him that resonance
of his charm invokes
my breathing,
Richness of his porous fingers
makes my core fall into
an immense wreathing.

Adieu to his soul
chaos in my ears,
And the wailing of my spirit
brings a storm so fierce.

O' Melancholy!
Do take me in your lap,
Where my eyes can rest into

a never ending nap.

The Silent Sea

O' silent sea!
Would you accept
my plea,
A coin is lost in you
A favour, wish you can do!

There is a shimmering
shine in that coin
Will you ask it
for me to join.

Tell that a metallic wave
waits outside,
Longing to take it to
another side.

Whisper it to melt in each other
So that we two can be a feather.

I Love My Emotions

I love my emotions
don't sprinkle sesame
over illusions,
I admit I feel so deep
that my being taught some
loyalty to keep.

I am not afraid of any truth
my belonging for every stone
is full of ruth,
I sniff in abundance
the flowers of my eyes
not falling for fragrance.

I can knit a nest
with my skin
where the fledgling can
fly and win,
Holding this chord
I do pray to my God.

That the hatchling
wouldn't be helpless
and the stones
wouldn't be restless.

Oh, how I love
my deep emotions,
as it does create
radiant transfigurations.

Ashes And Omens

Revoking Galatia guarding the bushes,
fabulous flowers turning into ashes.

Gibbering sounds floating in depths,
virtuous souls losing breaths.

Partially beasts eating humans,
grooving figs, bad omens.

Catalpa poking roving punches,
owls of death sitting in bunches.

Thanatos getting its prime deed,
freaking sheets laying over feed.

Drenching sky being bloody red,
breathing roses, withered fed.

Upon the shelter, prairie frogs,
all the roots having messy logs.

Silent In The Shroud

A golden hairy squirrel
jumped over the tree.

The black eyes of an eagle
trapped it to be eternally free

It kept on with its jump
the waiting eyes falling
for its golden slump.

When the squirrel came down
to take rest
the eyes caught it for its zest.

All the light it lost
in that crowd

And the black eyes left her
silent in the shroud.

Dorothy

O' Dorothy
when you come to me
chuckle the berries
of heavy thud.

Plums of wavering breath
deserve your honey ship.
Resting arms
crave your shivering touch.

O' Dorothy
my nerves growing dry
when will you come?

Pearl Of Hope

Falling into a dark well
a wish still echoes
in a seashell.

The pearls of hope
will shine a day
and thunder-lights
will sparkle the hay.

O' Ardour, be calm
don't mourn
see, the sheets
of prospects are not torn.

Wait for a while
till the entity does exile
let the day advent
when the pearls shall smile.

The Blue Roots

Weaving blue roots
in my navel
a grieving thread connects
silently like a pain.
The threads spining
around like a crystal ball
slowly churning nectar to be
my destiny's gain.

Cotton Dew

A musk wanted to wander
with the clouds to rain within
and fall like a cotton dew
to mist in the holy wind's begin.

Far, far later, a seed of soul originated
in the grounds of purity
and the wind nurtured it
through its enchanting gravity.

Gradually, the golden roots
began illuminating
and the wind embraced its glow
with a breath so animating.

Yearning Of Crude Breaths:
A Lesson Of The Void

Wearing sheets of tear
my skin melting in grip of fear.

Grasses of pain grooving
my brain frozen, not moving.

Pores of wisdom are blocked
I am left in anguish, deeply shocked.

All the glory burning in fire
leaving me in shrouded attire.

Crude breaths wanting to fly
learning the message
to be kind and wise.

Incarnation

An oath was taken
in a prophet's tomb
that incarnated
a blessing in a womb.

A wholeness was there
in that energy
which carved that soul
into a prodigy.

Fractured Echoes Behind
False Feelings

Lost the blinking
of his eyes
Smelled the goose
in the era of rise
Settled the symmetry
of clinking twice
Felt my amphalos
a truth so wise.

Oh, so messy my mind
There were many
reasons behind
Not a single thing
my heart could chase
As my soul was left
in a trembling phase.

Hide, spied, there was
nothing to be tied

Seeing all those voids
my echoes got crucified.

Screamed, trimmed
All my emotions
Were cut into strings
Oh! Almighty
My innerness is begging for
some spiritual springs.

My Fragile Bliss

Bells in tunnels
ringing for the drain
Rivers of love
waiting for the rain.

Oh! my fragile bliss
don't worry
The weather will harvest
the cherished grain
Warbling birds will dance
like jingles in the plain
And the timberlands will
light the twinkling brain.

Oh! my fragile bliss
don't shatter
The cosmos will create
an ethereal chain
And nature will get
its drifting soil again.

Your Footprints

Your footprints left over
the grass
planted a seed of
shining brass.

Once the stranger storm
brought the roil
the glimmers of the brass
refused to leave its soil.

The charm grew longer
and the seed gave birth
to a lampyrid much stronger.

Finally, the golden wings
unfurled in serenity
and started searching
footprint's couch till infinity!

Echoes Of Hidden Truth

Goose pricks
inside the streams
making tricks
over soothing dreams.

Lonesome hardy wearing
the hollow blindness
pure souls never
fearing to offer kindness.

Grigs of empathy
in their lowest form
letting the creed
tear the storm.

Deadly pruned stems
charming light
let us make the
loathsome into a kite.

Gothism will graze
the dreary goons
finding miracles
in freaky rooms.

Blind Faith Of A Puppet

The puppet had faith
in those fingers,
and an emotion that
often hinders.

My search for the holy potion
when all is gone in the air,
a long, hollow howl
is that still lingers.

The Haunting Darkness

Life-shivering
needles of Nyx
sobbing with
the blood moon
screams of torment
venomizing nectars
in the lagoon.

Bitter bugs
of deception
infesting luminous
oak tree
the spectre of
dismay clouds
scatter all over the glee.

Resurrecting My Being

O' Poesia!

Wrinkles in your heart
sculpt the wounds
so silently
the droplets of your cry
sound like a trumpet call
persistently.

O' Poesia!

How you mould
the breath of sorrow
into a golden chapel
bloomig softly
into my being
a moon-like dapple.

Bliss Of Love And Sorrow

*Trembling hum of
my restless pulse
running with your
untouched thread
of inner light,
Tied up with the bruises
of fire in agony.*

*Oh,
if it could be a thread of
inner light only
lest my heart should be
torn apart,
Yet your light of love
gets sealed into a
soul-crushing grief.*

*Oh,
how my heart drifts
from yours*

catching voliantly
the tides of sad eras,
With time it would feel
the deep bliss of
love and sorrow
both in abundance.

Ripples

The pearls in the
corners of my eyes
waiting to wrap
you around.
Persistence of my
melting ties
longing to hold your
celestial ground.
Oh, the union of my senses!
You are not made
to slump into cries
Open the ripples
of virgin sea.
Oh, my humming zinnia!
Wake up and chase
the deepest skies
and get the bunches
of drizzle's key.

Breathing Trinity

Breathing trinity
shatters before
the eyes of a dove
melting out its crest
like a proteus-cloned love.

An angel of mercy
blessing the cursed barrage
reuniting the surviving
fragments into
triune courage.

Slivers Of My Soul

Rappelling surge of dark
devouring globes
of my eyes
shoots of ashes
germinating hollow cries.

Black smoke
engulfing every nerve
Cerberus staring
to drain my verve.

Deep-set wounds
screaming
inside spooky thorns
slivers of my soul
being crushed
under the mourns.

A wisp of azalea
drifting across the sky

the God picking it
feeling every sordid sigh.

A drop of severance
fell into my heart
and lit up
peace in every part.

Carving The Ethereal Existence

Oh, my eyes
closed so deeply
thirsting to carve
your essence within.

The moon sheds
upon my bare soul
shaping a hollow sphere
in your absence.

The yearning lights of stars
falling to fade
Vast darkness sleeping
within my heart.

A piece of the sky
descending towards me
covering the saddened
breaths of mine.

Oh, my eyes
collecting the drops of
green radiance
waiting to honor your
ethereal existence.

My Inner Reeds

Recasting my nib's slit
creating a
thatching hut
where my inner reeds
can flute a soulful
harmonious song.

Song of Spirits
Song of Bliss
And Song of Nimbus!

Oh, how beautiful
the bows of
dew-laden grasses
the swaying ice-fogs
talking to wandering birds
and passing
the breezy
soothing letters.

Letters to my voice
Letters to my silence
And Letters to my crest!

Being Awaken

Maples of honey wind
tearing my
healed-wounded wing,
just to find a voice
that gathers
the flowers to sing.

Muddy, drowsy dogs
barking to call
the companions
of the dark,
Intense, buried ecstasy
bowing beneath
a sharp, miserable arc.

Vivid shadows of
negligence
stirring my raw emotions
to quake,
a simple thought of

diving deep
would soothe my soul
and make it awake.

The Blue Hue

The impression of
your soul
on my soul is like
the blue hue of
Lord Shiva's throat
leading to eternity till
the universe throbs
and even thereafter.

Hallucinating Hemlock

Once the hemlock's love
cuddles
no stream allows you
to swim across.

And the dark
illuminations lead you
towards the
death cave of
blue frozen petals.

Oh yes, your veins
would float
in the mines of
flesh coal.

And your pulse
shall stuck in the
hallucination of
lurking revenants.

The Waves Of Infinity

A rose petal said to
the honey bee
do take my essence
and let me die.

But don't forget to carry me
to the sacred cave
where I may mist into
the waves of infinity.

The Last Hope

Some souls find theirs
and some do not
doesn't mean the absence
of closeness or soreness.

The feeling echoes
in eternity
like butterfly wings
fluttering unstoppably
tired of not hearing
the other side's voice.

Getting dry and fading
its colors
taking last breath
in the hope of some depth.

Ocean Of Tears

Let my tears make
the deepest ocean
for you to be lost within
After eras
when you ache
with my absence in your core
Find me
through my inner whispers
carrying the seeds
of becoming one
And let your thirst
inhale the whole ocean
within you
and hold it forever.

The Fragrant Dream

Running veins in sticky fans
breezy breath
prickly chains.
Oh, his dreams!
taking me in the flurry crest
laying me gently
on his bare chest.

Oh, his exhalation!
cuddling me in his arm
swaying my eyes
in blissful calm.

Oh, his fragrant embrace!
singing like jasmine
under the pearly moon
plucking the birds of sleep
carrying me into swoon.

Oh, his dreams!

being brighter with the
night-blooming flowers
refusing to rise
surrendering to sleep
over long hours.

Sobbing Rain

Gingerly prior
occurrences
in booths of chaos
inside one's fragments
Overwhelming
the galaxy with the
strongly-provocative posture
of one's moon
Do you ever feel
all these overwhelming
and chaotic pains within
full of hangs
Grievous of understanding
no one believes that
certain peacocks
drenching in sobbing rain
If one catches these
to inhale
God shall honour one
in the universe of Plutus.

Transparent Sheets

Closing my eyes,
emotions shrink deep
and send a wind
guarded with love
The purity of eyelids
forms transparent sheets of
inhale and exhale
The wind passes again,
the love, coated with
breezy breaths.

Wandering Miracle

Miracle happens
with the tinny torn heart
drooped in a wanderlust park.

Miracle happens
wheezing roots
of empathy falls in dark.

Miracle happens
with choosy grunts
seeding in bruised bark.

Miracle happens
grazing the empty fungus
in the mouth of shark.

Miracle happens
with the bloody, guarded
anxiety of painful arc.

Silver Moon

Find me beyond the
rays of a sterling
silver moon
where we exist
like the couplet
of a rhyme
Falling asleep
in the sky of
dazed emotions
where starlight covers
us with their
flourished-graced blanket.

The Picture of Love

Have you ever heard
the voice of melting sand?
Sand, that flows into
your eyes and brain,

Sings the song of
a smouldering heart,
Keeps you sprinting towards
the picture of love,
Enfolds you in the colors
of silent throbs.

Restless Persuit

At the pebbles of a
Falling waterfall
I saw you standing
And heard your whispers
In my ears about a will
To awaken my spirit
Within me.

By the lonesome sea shore
I saw you carve
a sleeping seed
With sacred waves
Asking me to nurture it
To give it a shape for my soul.

In the silent streets
I saw you walking alone
Under the street lights
Watching me to listen
The call of my inner self.

But my soul still asks
Why you bid adieu without
Saying a final word
My soul still searches for you
In restless pursuit.

Cryptic Trace

Do take a while
To know who lies besides you
when falling into
a deep sleep

Do take a while
To know who resides around you
While sparking fire
in solitude

Do take a while
To choose who you believe
And let not your emotions
Fall away from the path

Do take a while
Before your soul spills out
For a false cryptic trace.

Love Aches Of The Past

Oh, that innocent love
of my childhood!
Why you still long for
tenderness lost in the past?

Oh, the tempered love
of my teen!
Why do your broken seeds sprout
A cactus in my fields of dreams?

Oh, the enduring love
of my later years!
Be calm, you deserve some
lustrous jasmines in your garden.

Shaping The Ally Of Light

I am not alone.
My distortions shaping me
with motionless fortitude.

I am not alone.
My sensory pathways meet the
fused resilience to rekindle.

I am not alone.
My miseries of fragrant soul
chisel the ally of light.

Whispers Of Unheard Vibrations

Pearly frozen mountains
radiating from my core
towards your galaxy
Longing to be
engrossed in your
vibrant omphalos

Half chewed nails give
a sign of twilight
Throbbing with your
ambience of
respiratory veins
And thinking of
being crumpled
like autumn leaves.

O' listen to the voice of
unheard vibrations
The blooming

fragrance of
snow white mountains
And take my palette of soul
Absorbing all the
floating colors in your granules.

Unhealed Faith

Holding my inner urn
upside down,
not to pour,
but to show
how much of me
became emptied,
bleeding
in the ache of half-lit faith.

An ocean's soul
never stayed
to see the cracks
of my devotion's drop.

I gave,
not water,
not wine,
not any premium potion,
but the pieces
of my core.

Still,
it was not enough
to make it whole.

I could have stitched
every wave of it
with my skin,
so much sacrifice
was there
inside my womb.

Betrayed Equations

Isn't it easy to believe
while wandering
in wind
chasing meanings
some echoes stayed.

Not for being heard
but to remember
how gently
some phrases
rested between
verses of heart.

May be it meant
to be lived once
as if it was
never spoken
just breathed in
and left behind
in the space

between two pauses.

What a
balancing equation
It is to be!

Luminous Aether

Beneath the falling skies
I didn't just see
the waterfall
I saw memories,
promises
and silent prayers
dissolving into aether.

Turbulent Soul

Between euphoria
and agonizing pain
my soul's lament is
only an aching rain

My wilted heart paints you
as a blood red rose
As I try hard to capture
the stillness in a happy pose.

Does love need to
end and just bleed
O' life why don't you sprout
in me a living seed!

www.ingramcontent.com/pod-product-compliance
Lightning Source LLC
Chambersburg PA
CBHW060349050426
42449CB00011B/2894

9 781807 153526